Dr. Crisp Media Center
50 Arlington Street
Nashua, NH 03060

Scarecrows

by Lola M. Schaefer

Consulting Editor:
Gail Saunders-Smith, Ph.D.

Consultant:
Terry Kuseske
National Council for
the Social Studies

Pebble Books

an imprint of Capstone Press
Mankato, Minnesota

Pebble Books are published by Capstone Press
818 North Willow Street, Mankato, Minnesota 56001
http://www.capstone-press.com

Library of Congress Cataloging-in-Publication Data
Schaefer, Lola M., 1950–
    Scarecrows/by Lola M. Schaefer.
      p. cm.—(Fall fun)
    Includes bibliographical references (p. 23) and index.
    Summary: Simple text and photographs describe scarecrows, their purpose,
composition, and places where they are found.
    ISBN 0-7368-0107-3
    1. Scarecrows—Juvenile literature. [1. Scarecrows.] I. Title. II. Series: Schaefer,
Lola M. 1950– Fall fun.
SB995.25.S35   1999
632'.68—dc21   98-23269
                                                                          CIP
                                                                          AC

Note to Parents and Teachers

This series supports units on fall celebrations. This book describes
and illustrates scarecrows and where they are used. The
photographs support emergent readers in understanding the text.
Repetition of words and phrases helps emergent readers learn new
words. This book introduces emergent readers to vocabulary used
in this subject area. The vocabulary is defined in the Words to Know
section. Emergent readers may need assistance in reading some
words and in using the Table of Contents, Words to Know, Read
More, Internet Sites, and Index/Word List sections of the book.

Table of Contents

Parts of Scarecrows 5

Places for Scarecrows 15

What Scarecrows Do 19

Note to Parents and Teachers . . . 2

Words to Know 22

Read More 23

Internet Sites 23

Index/Word List 24

Scarecrows are
straw people.

Old hats cover
straw heads.

Old shirts cover
straw arms.

Old pants cover
straw legs.

Old boots cover
straw feet.

Some scarecrows stand
in fields.

Some scarecrows stand in gardens.

Scarecrows frighten
birds away

sometimes.

Words to Know

field—an area of land used for growing crops

frighten—to scare

straw—dried stems of wheat, barley, or oat plants

Read More

Littlewood, Valerie. *Scarecrow!* New York: Dutton Children's Books, 1992.

Martin, Bobi. *All about Scarecrows.* Fairfield, Calif.: Tomato Enterprises, 1990.

Rylant, Cynthia. *Scarecrow.* San Diego: Harcourt Brace, 1998.

Internet Sites

Paperbag Scarecrow
http://tac.shopnetmall.com/www.funroom.com/halloween/scarecrow.html

Scarecrow
http://family.disney.com/Categories/Activities/Features/family_0401_01/dony/donyout_art/donyout256.html

Scarecrow Day!
http://mrsburns.simplenet.com/scare2.htm

Index/Word List

are, 5
arms, 9
away, 19
birds, 19
boots, 13
cover, 7, 9, 11, 13
feet, 13
fields, 15
frighten, 19
gardens, 17
hats, 7

heads, 7
legs, 11
old, 7, 9, 11, 13
pants, 11
people, 5
scarecrows, 5, 15, 17, 19
shirts, 9
some, 15, 17
sometimes, 21
stand, 15, 17
straw, 5, 7, 9, 11, 13

Word Count: 39
Early-Intervention Level: 5

Editorial Credits

Martha Hillman, editor; Clay Schotzko/Icon Productions, cover designer;
Sheri Gosewisch, photo researcher

Photo Credits

Betty Crowell, 12, 18
Chuck Place, 8
Image West/Carolyn Fox, 1
Jack MacFarlane, 6
James P. Rowan, 20
Photobank Inc./Kent Knudson, 10
Unicorn Stock Photos/Chuck Schmeiser, 14; Margaret Finefrock, 16
Visuals Unlimited/Arthur R. Hill, cover; Mark E. Gibson, 4

632
SCH

Schaefer, Lola M.
Scarecrows

PERMA-BOUND. BAR: 1000710074

DATE DUE			